About this book:

The Language Bear's dual-language books are self-directed learning and are specifically designed to help young children better understand foreign words and phrases. The teaching methods used in this book allow children to learn at their own pace and enjoy the learning process. These methods include:

Repeat words

Simple phrases

Opposites

Highlighted vocab words

Contextual learning

Corresponding imagery

Find more dual-language books at: **www.theLanguageBear.com**

Dedicated to all those with a
passion for knowledge.
There is no end to learning,
but there are many beginnings.

The Language Bear Bilingual Books
207-370-4298
info@theLanguageBear.com
www.theLanguageBear.com

The Adventures of Bosley Bear
Bosley Sees the World

Written by: Tim Johnson

Translated by: Orlando Soto

Illustrated by: Ozzy Esha

Bosley Bear woke up one morning in his cozy little cave.
He stretched his front paws.
He stretched his back paws.

Oso Bosley despertó una mañana en su cuevita cómoda.
Estiró sus patas de adelante.
Estiró sus patas de atrás.

Bosley looked around and said, "Mama, we have such a tiny cave. I've seen everything in this cave..."

Bosley miró a su alrededor y dijo: "Mamá, tenemos una cueva tan pequeñita. He visto todo en esta cueva..."

"I'll explore outdoors!" Bosley decided.
He ran out of the cave.
He ran into the forest.

"¡Exploraré afuera!" decidió Bosley.
Salió corriendo de la cueva.
Corrió hasta entrar al bosque.

Bosley looked around..
"This tree is very tall!"
He looked up at the branches.
He looked down at the roots.
"I'll climb to the top!" thought Bosley

Bosley miró a su alrededor.
"¡Este árbol es muy alto!"
Miró arriba hacia las ramas.
Miró abajo hacia las raíces.
"¡Subiré hasta la punta!" pensó Bosley.

From the top of the tree,
Bosley Bear shouted,
"This forest is so big!"

Desde la punta del árbol,
Oso Bosley exclamó:
"¡Este bosque es tan grande!"

He heard birds singing high above his head.
He heard a river rushing through the forest.
"I'll run to the other side of the forest!"

Oyó pájaros cantando por encima de su cabeza.
Oyó un río corriendo a través del bosque.
"¡Voy a correr hasta el otro lado del bosque!"

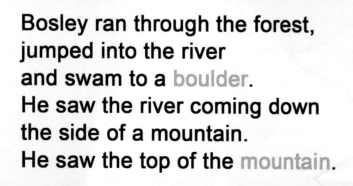

Bosley ran through the forest,
jumped into the river
and swam to a boulder.
He saw the river coming down
the side of a mountain.
He saw the top of the mountain.

Bosley corrió por el bosque,
brincó dentro del río
y nadó hasta un peñón.
Vio cómo el río bajaba por
el costado de la montaña
Vio la cima de la montaña.

It was so tall.
It was so far away.
"I can climb that mountain!"
Bosley decided.

Era tan alta.
Estaba tan lejos.
"¡Yo puedo escalar esa montaña!"
Bosley decidió.

He shook off his wet fur and ran toward the mountain.
He looked up at the top of the mountain.
The mountain was much taller than the tree.
The mountain was much bigger than the forest.

Se sacudió el pelaje mojado y corrió hacia la montaña.
Miró arriba hacia la cima de la montaña.
La montaña era mucho más alta que el árbol.
La montaña era mucho más grande que el bosque.

When Bosley reached the highest point he stopped and sat down.
He could see the river.
He looked at the big forest, and he looked at the tall trees.
He could see his tiny cave in the distance.

Cuando Bosley llegó a la cima, se detuvo y se sentó.
Podía ver el río.
Miró el bosque grande y miró los árboles altos.
Podía ver su pequeña cueva en la distancia.

And then he saw so much more that he hadn't explored yet, and he wondered, "How is it that the world can be so big?? I have so much to explore!"

Entonces vio mucho más que aún no había explorado y se preguntó: "¿Cómo es que el mundo puede ser tan grande? ¡Tengo tanto que explorar!"

"But that will have to wait until another day.
It's too big for me now."
And Bosley walked back to his tiny cave.

"Pero eso tendrá que
esperar hasta otro día.
Es demasiado grande para
mí ahora mismo".
Y Bosley caminó de regreso
a su pequeña cueva.

It was the perfect size for Bosley.
He curled up in his little bed and
dreamed about the big world.
He would explore it all someday.
He knew it.

Era del tamaño perfecto para Bosley.
Se acurrucó en su camita
y soñó con ese gran mundo.
Lo exploraría todo algún día.
Lo sabía.

The End
Fin

New Words (Palabras nuevas):

Adventure
Aventura

World
Mundo

to See
Ver

Morning
Mañana

Cave
Cueva

to Stretch
(as in, to stretch one's own body)
Estirar

to Explore
Explorar

to Run
Correr

Tree
Árbol

to Look
Mirar

to Climb
(as in, to climb a tree)
Subir

to Climb
(as in, to climb a mountain)
Escalar

Forest
Bosque

to Hear
Oír

Bird
Pájaro

River
Río

Mountain
Montaña

to Dream
(as in, a dream during sleep)
Soñar

This book was made possible by:

Richard and Joan Legendre

Ray Legendre

Michael and Sarah Governale

Masa

Hiiro Hiromi and Daisuke

Quentin and Tara Abraham

All of Bosley's friends,

And You!

Thank you for supporting The Language Bear and bilingual education!

Find more dual-language children's books at:

www.theLanguageBear.com